MY SiDEWALKS ON
SCOTT FORESMAN
READING STREET
Intensive Reading Intervention

Practice Book
Teacher's Manual

Level
A

PEARSON
Scott
Foresman

Glenview, Illinois • Boston, Massachusetts • Chandler, Arizona
Upper Saddle River, New Jersey

ISBN-13:   978-0-328-45372-6
ISBN-10:   0-328-45372-2

8 9 10 V069 15 14 13

Contents

Name_____

Say the word for each picture.
Circle the picture if the word begins
with the **m** sound heard in **mat**.

<u>m</u>at

1.

2.

3.

4.

5.

6.

7.

8.

9.
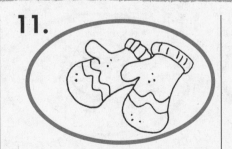

10.

11.

12.

© Pearson Education A

Name _____

Say the word for each picture.
Circle the picture if the word begins
with the **t** sound heard in **table**.

<u>t</u>able

1.

2.

3.

4.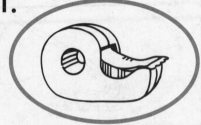

5.

6.

7.

8.

9.

10.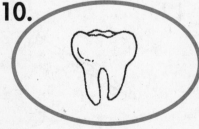

11.

12.

School + Home

Home Activity This page practices words that have the *t* sound heard in *tag*. Work through the items with your child. As you read with your child, encourage him or her to point out words that begin with the *t* sound.

Name_____

Say the word for each picture.
Write a on the line if you hear the
short **a** sound heard in **mat**.

m<u>a</u>t

1. c <u>**a**</u> t

2. f ____ sh

3. p <u>**a**</u> n

4. b <u>**a**</u> t

5. s ____ n

6. b <u>**a**</u> g

7. l ____ d

8. c <u>**a**</u> p

Say the word for each picture.
Find the picture that has the same middle sound as .
Mark the ⬭ to show your answer.

9.

10.

School + Home **Home Activity** This page practices words that have the short a sound heard in *tap*. Work through the items with your child. Help your child make up fun rhymes using short a words, such as: *The fat cat in the black hat sat on the mat.*

Phonics Aa, Short a **3**

Name_____

Pick a word from the box to finish each sentence.
Write the word on the line.

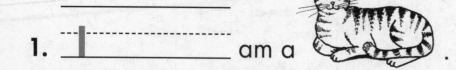

| I | like | the |

1. **I**_____ am a 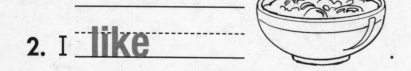 .

2. I **like**_____ 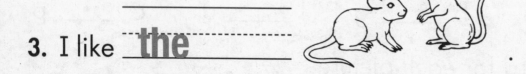 .

3. I like **the**_____ 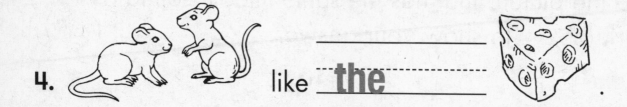 .

4. _____ like **the**_____ 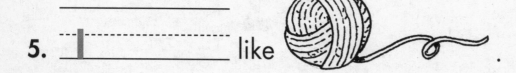 .

5. **I**_____ like .

© Pearson Education A

Name_____

Finish each sentence.
Write the words on the lines.

Possible answers:

1. _____ like **bones** .

2. _____ like **to sleep** .

3. _____ like **to swim** .

4. I like **pizza** .

5. I like **to read** .

© Pearson Education A

 Home Activity This page helps your child finish sentences and learn to write sentences. Help your child write the sentences. Then ask your child the things he or she may have in common with a pet, such as *like to play* and *need food and love.*

Name_____

Say the word for each picture.
Circle the picture if the word begins
with the **s** sound heard in **seven**.

<u>s</u>even

1.

2.

3.

4.

5.

6.
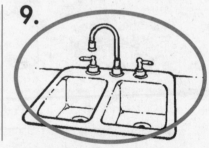

7.

8.

9.

10.

11.
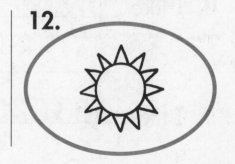

12.

 School + Home **Home Activity** This page practices words that have the *s* sound heard in *soup*. Work through the items with your child. Then say aloud groups of three words, such as *cold, left,* and *safe*. Ask your child to listen carefully and name the word with the *s* sound.

© Pearson Education A

Name_____

Say the word for each picture.
Circle the picture if the word begins
with the **p** sound heard in **pat**.   <u>p</u>at

 School + Home **Home Activity** This page practices words that have the *p* sound heard in *pink*. Work through the items with your child. Then act out words beginning with the *p* sound, such as *pig, pail, pat,* and *pet,* and have your child guess the word.

Name_____

Say the word for each picture.
Circle the word.

T**i**m

---

1.  (map) pit

2.  (sit) mat

---

3.  pat (mitt)

4.  (sip) Sam

---

Say the word for each picture.
Find the picture that has the same middle sound as .
Mark the ⬭ to show your answer.

5. ⬭ ▬ ⬭

6. ⬭ ⬭ ▬

---

7. ▬ ⬭ ⬭

8. ▬ ⬭ ⬭

 Home Activity This page practices words that have the short *i* sound heard in *ship*. Work through the items with your child. Have your child use the short *i* words pictured above in sentences.

© Pearson Education A

Name_____

Pick a word from the box to finish each sentence.
Write it on the line.

| a | is | look |

1. Pip __is_____ a  .

2. Pip likes __a_____  .

3. Pam __is_____ a .

4. I __look_____ at Pam.

5. I __look_____ at Pip.

 School + Home

Home Activity This page helps your child learn to read and write the words *a*, *is*, and *look*. Work through the items with your child. Then help your child use these sentence frames to make more sentences: *Look at (name). (Name) is a _____.*

Name_____

Finish each sentence.
Write the words on the lines.

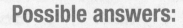

Possible answers:

1. A _____ is <u>a doctor for animals</u> _____ .

2. A _____ looks at <u>sick pets</u> _____ .

3. A _____ likes <u>to help animals</u> _____ .

4. I <u>can wash a pet</u> _____ .

5. I <u>can feed a pet</u> _____ .

Home Activity This page helps your child finish sentences and learn to write sentences. Help your child write the sentences. Then ask your child to tell some ways he or she can help animals at home or at a shelter.

Name_____

Look for **C** and **c**.
Circle them.

Cc

1. D Ⓒ O   **2.** B G Ⓒ

3. ⓒ g e   **4.** o ⓒ p

Say the word for each picture.
Write c if you hear the sound of **c** heard in **camel**.

5.

_____

- - - - - - - - - - - - - - - - - - - -

6.

_____

- - - - - - - - c - - - - - -

7.

_____

- - - - - - - c - - - - - - -

8.

_____

- - - - - - - c - - - - - - -

9.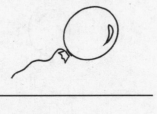

_____

- - - - - - - - - - - - - - - - - - - -

10.

_____

- - - - - - - c - - - - - - -

Home Activity This page practices recognizing the letter Cc and identifying the sound of c heard in *cut*.
Say these words one at a time: *come, big, cake, cap, me*. Have your child stand up if the word starts with c.

Name _____

Look for **B** and **b**.
Circle them.

Bb

1. (B) P D   2. E R (B)

3. p (b) q   4. d g (b)

Say the word for each picture.
Write b if you hear the sound of **b** heard in **bus**.

5.

_____
- - - - - - **b** - - - - - -

6.

_____
- - - - - - **b** - - - - - -

7.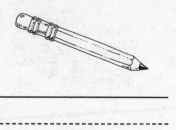

_____
- - - - - - - - - - - -

8.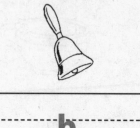

_____
- - - - - - **b** - - - - - -

9.

_____
- - - - - - - - - - - -

10.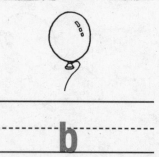

_____
- - - - - - **b** - - - - - -

School + Home

Home Activity This page practices recognizing the letter *Bb* and identifying the sound of *b* heard in *ball*.
Work through the items with your child. Then help your child look at home for three things that begin with *b*.

© Pearson Education A

Name_____

Look for **O** and **o**.
Circle them.   **Oo**

1. C Ⓞ G   **2.** P Q Ⓞ

3. g ⓞ c   **4.** ⓞ e d

Write o on each line.
Say the word you made.
Draw a line to the picture it matches.   c**o**t

5. m ___**0**___ p

6. p ___**0**___ t

7. t ___**0**___ p

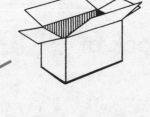

8. b ___**0**___ x

Home Activity This page practices recognizing the letter *Oo* and identifying the short *o* sound heard in *box*.
Work through the items with your child. Then have your child spell these words: *top, Tom, mom, pot, Bob.*

© Pearson Education A

Name_____

Circle a word to finish each sentence.
Write it on the line.

(We)   Have

_____

1. ___**We**___ look.

(have)   you

_____

2. I ___**have**___ the cat.

(have)   we

_____

3. I ___**have**___ the bat.

we   (you)

_____

4. I look at ___**you**___ .

Have   (We)

_____

5. ___**We**___ like the top.

 School + Home **Home Activity** This page helps your child learn to read and write the words *have, you,* and *we.* Work through the items with your child. Then help your child make up sentences using the words *have, you,* and *we.*

© Pearson Education A

Name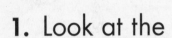

Think about how animals can help.
Finish the sentences.   **Answers will vary.**

1. Look at the .

_____

It can give eggs.   .

2. Look at the  .

_____

It can give milk.   .

3. Look at the  .

_____

It can give wool.   .

4. Look at the  .

_____

It can walk with us.   .

Home Activity This page helps your child learn to write sentences. Name each picture on the page. Then help your child write the sentences. Read the sentences together.

© Pearson Education A

Name_____

Look for **N** and **n**.
Circle them.

Nn

1. A (N) W   2. (N) M H

3. m u (n)   4. h (n) r

Say the word for each picture.
Write n if you hear the sound of **n** heard in **nickel**.

5.
_____
- - - - - - - - - - -

6.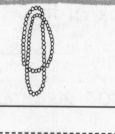
_____
- - - - n - - - - -

7.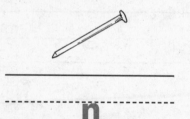
_____
- - - - n - - - - -

8.
_____
- - - - - - - - - - -

9.
_____
- - - - n - - - - -

10.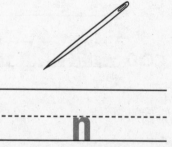
_____
- - - - n - - - - -

 Home Activity This page practices recognizing the letter Nn and identifying the sound of n heard in *nurse*. For fun, let your child try saying this sentence quickly: *Nan needs nine nuts.* Then have him or her replace *nuts* with other words that begin with *n*.

Name_____

Look for **D** and **d.**
Circle them.

Dd

1. P R Ⓓ   2. B O Ⓓ

3. p ⓓ g   4. ⓓ q b

Say the word for each picture. **Find** the picture that has
the same beginning sound as .
Mark the ⬭ to show your answer.

5.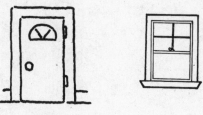

6.

7.

8.

9.

10.

Home Activity This page practices recognizing the letter *Dd* and identifying the sound of *d* heard in *dime*.
Say the following words one at a time, and have your child say a rhyming word that begins with the *d* sound:
not, keep, may, rip. (*dot, deep, day, dip*)

Practice Book Unit 1   **Phonics** *Dd/d/* **17**

Name_____

Look for **R** and **r**.
Circle them.   **Rr**

1. B P Ⓡ   2. Ⓡ D V

3. ⓡ n m   4. v h ⓡ

Say the word for each picture. **Find** the picture that
has the same beginning sound as .
Mark the ⬭ to show your answer.

5.
   ⬭   ▬   ⬭

6.
   ⬭   ⬭   ▬

7.
   ▬   ⬭   ⬭

8.
   ⬭   ▬   ⬭

 Home Activity This page practices recognizing the letter *Rr* and identifying the sound of *r* heard in *radio*.
Say these pairs of words, and have your child say the word beginning with *r*: walk/run, rake/hoe, read/talk.
Let your child act out the *r* word.

© Pearson Education A

Name_____

Pick a word from the box to finish each sentence.
Write it on the line.

> **are** **little** **see**

1. We __**are**__ on a mat.

2. We __**see**__ an ant.

3. The ant is __**little**__ .

4. We __**see**__ Dad.

5. Dad is not __**little**__ .

School + Home **Home Activity** This page helps your child learn to read and write the words *are*, *little*, and *see*. Work through the items together. Then write each word on a card. Lay the cards face down. Have your child pick up the cards and read the words.

Name

Finish each sentence. The words in the box may help you. **Write** the words on the lines.

sit   mat   nap   bib   little

1. I see _____ .

The _____ are on a ___ mat ___ .

2. I see _____ .

The _____ have a ___ bib ___ .

3. I see _____ .

The _____ are ___ little ___ .

4. I see _____ .

The _____ ___ sit ___ in a _____ .

5. I see _____ .

The _____ ___ nap ___ .

 Home Activity This page helps your child practice writing sentences to describe animals. Help your child write the sentences. Then read them together. Have your child say a sentence describing another animal he or she has seen.

© Pearson Education A

Name_____

Look for **K** and **k**. Circle them.

Kk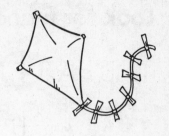

1. V Ⓚ F   2. Ⓚ H N

3. l ⓚ h   4. f y ⓚ

Say the word for each picture.
Find the picture that has
the same beginning sound as .
Mark the ⬭ to show your answer.

5.

6.

7.

8.

Home Activity This page practices recognizing the letter *Kk* and identifying the sound of *k* heard in *kitten*. Name each picture. Work through the items with your child. Say the following words one at a time, and have your child say a rhyming word that begins with *k*: mitten, hid, fit, miss. (*kitten, kid, kit, kiss*)

Name_____

Look for **F** and **f**. **Circle** them.

Ff

1. E A (F)   2. P (F) B

3. (f) k b   4. d h (f)

Say the word for each picture.
Find the picture that has
the same beginning sound as  .
Mark the ⬭ to show your answer.

5.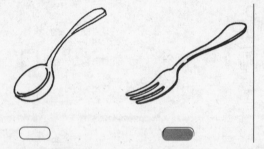
⬭   ⬭

6.
⬭   ⬭

7. 5   7
⬭   ⬭

8.
⬭   ⬭

9.
⬭   ⬭

10.
⬭   ⬭

© Pearson Education A

 Home Activity This page practices recognizing the letter *Ff* and identifying the sound of *f* heard in *finger*.
School + Home Name each picture. Work through the items with your child. Then walk through your home with your child
and ask him or her to point out things that begin with the *f* sound.

Name_____

Look for **E** and **e**.
Circle them.

Ee

1. (E) F P   2. B (E) R

3. (e) c o   4. b g (e)

Write e on each line.
Say the word you made.
Draw a line to the picture it matches.

h**e**n

5. b ___**e**___ d

6. p ___**e**___ n

7. n ___**e**___ t

8. t ___**e**___ n

© Pearson Education **A**

 School + Home **Home Activity** This page practices recognizing the letter *Ee* and identifying the short e sound heard in *hen*. Work through the items with your child. Then write these words and ask your child to read them: *fed, met, pet, red, ten.*

Circle a word to finish each sentence.
Write it on the line.

(go)　　　he

_____

1. Look at Min **go** !

they　　　(go)

_____

2. Look at Tom **go** !

He　　　(They)

_____

3. **They** run and run.

(They)　　　Go

_____

4. **They** sit on a mat.

Go　　　(He)

_____

5. **He** can fan Min.

Home Activity This page helps your child learn to read and write the words *go, he,* and *they.* Write *he, they, go, He, They,* and *Go* on cards. Lay the cards face down. Have your child pick up the cards one at a time and read each word.

Name_____

Look at each picture. **Pick** a word from the box to finish each sentence. **Write** the word on the line.

> **bed   fan   mat   net   pot**

1. I look on the __mat__ .

   I see a 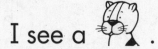 .

2. I look at the __net__ .

   I see a 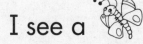 .

3. I look on the __bed__ .

   I see a 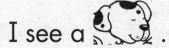 .

4. I look in the __pot__ .

   I see a 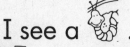 .

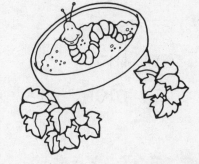

 Home Activity This page helps your child finish sentences. After your child writes the missing words, read all the sentences together. Have your child say one more sentence for each picture.

© Pearson Education A

Practice Book Unit 1   **Writing** **25**

Name_____

Say the word for each picture.
Circle the word.

hen

---

1.  (hit) **2.**  hot

  has (hat)

---

3.  hip **4.**  (hop)

  (hand) his

---

5. (ham)   **6.**   (hot)

  him hem

Find the word that has the same beginning sound
as  . **Mark** the ⬭ to show your answer.

7. ⬭ hid **8.** ⬭ bad
  ⬭ fit ⬭ red
  ⬭ not ⬭ had

9. ⬭ sip **10.** ⬭ mad
  ⬭ him ⬭ hen
  ⬭ men ⬭ tap

 School + Home **Home Activity** This page practices words that have the *h* sound heard in *home*. Work through the items with your child. Then say aloud groups of three words, such as *ten*, *head*, and *mend*. Ask your child to listen carefully and name the word with the *h* sound.

Name_____

Say the word for each picture.
Circle the picture if the word has
the **l** sound heard in **lid**.

<u>l</u>id →

1.

2.

3.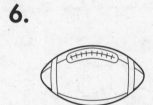

4.

5.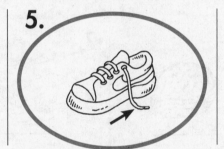

6.

7.

8.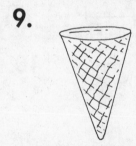

9.

10.

11.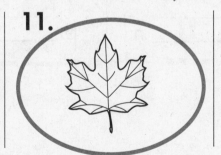

12.

 School + Home **Home Activity** This page practices words that have the *l* sound heard in *light*. Work through the items with your child. Work together to write silly sentences using as many *l* words as possible. For example: *The laughing lizard licked the little lime.*

Name _____

Say the word for each picture.
Write u on the line if you hear the
short **u** sound heard in **bus**.

b<u>u</u>s

1.

c __**u**__ t

2.

s __**u**__ n

3.

n _____ st

4.

t __**u**__ b

5.

c _____ p

6.

n __**U**__ t

7.

m __**U**__ d

8.

b _____ nd

9.

p __**U**__ p

10.

b __**U**__ n

11.

p _____ t

12.

h __**U**__ t

© Pearson Education A

School + Home

Home Activity This page practices words that have the short *u* sound heard in *bug*. Work through the items with your child. Invite your child to write or say words that rhyme with *sun*.

Name_____

Pick a word from the box to finish each sentence.
Write it on the line.

| Do | of | She |

1. Fen sees lots **of** _____ .

2. **She** _____ looks at the _____ .

3. **Do** _____ the  see Fen?

4. Fen likes the skin **of** _____ the  .

5. **She** _____ likes the  best.

Home Activity This page helps your child learn to read and write the words *do, of,* and *she.* Work through the items with your child. Then help your child think of questions about animals that begin with the word *do.*

Name_____

Finish each sentence.
Write the words on the lines.

Possible answers:

1. We can help __lions_____ .

2. We can __give them food_____ .

3. We can help __dogs_____ .

4. We can __give them baths_____ .

5. Draw a picture of one way you can help animals.

Pictures will vary but should show the child helping an animal.

© Pearson Education A

Home Activity This page helps your child practice writing sentences. Work with your child to write the sentences. Then have your child name one kind of wild animal. Talk about different ways people might help this animal.

Name_____

Pick letters from the box to finish each word.
Write the letters on the line.   <u>sl</u>ip

| fl | cl | cr | dr | sk | gr | sl | st | pl | sp |

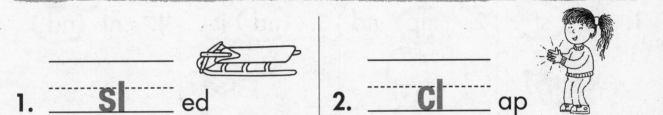

1. _____ **sl** ___ ed

2. _____ **cl** ___ ap

3. _____ **sp** ___ ot

4. _____ **sk** ___ ip

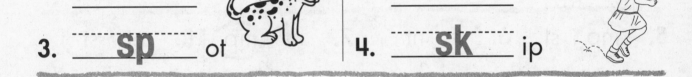

5. _____ **fl** ___ ag

6. _____ **st** ___ ar

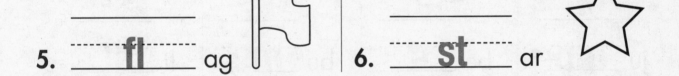

7. _____ **cr** ___ ab

8. _____ **gr** ___ in

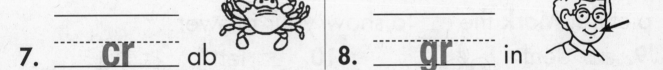

9. _____ **dr** ___ ip

10. _____ **pl** ___ um

© Pearson Education A

Name_____

Say the word for each picture.
Circle the letters that finish each word.
Write the letters on the line.   te**nt**

---

1. nt (st)

ne __**st**__

2. (mp) nd
la __**mp**__

3. (nd) lt
po __**nd**__

4. nt (nd)
ha __**nd**__

---

5. (mp) st
ju __**mp**__

6. (lt) nt
be __**lt**__

7. nt (mp)
bu __**mp**__

8. nt (st)
li __**st**__

Find the word that has the same ending sound as the picture. **Mark** the ⬭ to show your answer.

9. ⬭ dent
  ⬭ last
  ⬭ sand

10. ⬭ left
  ⬭ fast
  ⬭ bend

School + Home **Home Activity** This page practices words with final consonant blends, such as *want, best,* and *land.* Work through the items with your child. Have your child make up sentences using words from this page.

Name_____

Say the word for each picture.
Circle the picture if the word begins
with the **g** sound heard in **goat**.

<u>g</u>oat

1.

2.

3.

4.
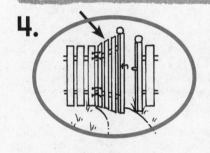

5.

6.

7.

8.

9.

10.

11.
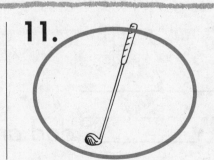

12.
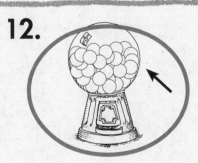

© Pearson Education A

School + Home **Home Activity** This page practices words that have the g sound heard in *good*. Work through the items with your child. Invite him or her to find objects in your home that begin with the g sound.

Name_____

Pick a word from the box to finish each sentence.
Write it on the line.

> here   to   my

_____
1. My dad is __**here**__ .

_____
2. We like __**to**__ fish in the pond.

_____
3. Here is __**my**__ mom.

_____
4. We like __**to**__ plant.

_____
5. My mom and __**my**__ dad are fun!

© Pearson Education A

School + Home **Home Activity** This page helps your child learn to read and write the words *here, to,* and *my*. Work through the items with your child. Then have your child use the words *my* and *to* in sentences that tell things he or she likes doing with your family.

Name_____

Finish each sentence.
Write the words on the lines.

What does your family do together? **Possible answers:**

1. We like to ___**play games**_____ .

2. We like to ___**eat dinner**_____ .

3. We go to ___**the park**_____ .

4. We go to ___**the zoo**_____ .

5. Draw a picture of your family. **Pictures will vary.**

© Pearson Education A

School + Home   **Home Activity** This page helps your child finish sentences and learn to write sentences. Help your child write the sentences. Then ask your child his or her favorite things to do with your family. Plan a special family trip together!

Name_____

Say the word for each picture.
Write w on the line if you hear the **w** sound heard in **well**.

<u>w</u>ell

1.

W et

2.

W ig

3.

_____ rog

4.

W eb

5.

W ind

6.

W ag

7.

_____ an

8.

_____ en

Find the word that begins with the **w** sound heard in ⊞.
Mark the ⬭ to show your answer.

9. ⬭ mask
   ⬤ will
   ⬭ fist

10. ⬭ flag
    ⬭ bell
    ⬤ went

School + Home **Home Activity** This page practices words that have the *w* sound heard in *west*. Work through the items with your child. Then work with him or her to make words that rhyme with *will* and *wig*.

Name_____

Say the word for each picture.
Circle the picture if the word begins with
the **j** sound heard in **jet**.

j̲et

| 1.  | 2.  | 3.  | 4. 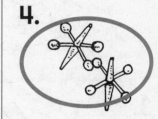 |

| 5. | 6.  | 7.  | 8.  |

Pick a word from the box to finish each sentence.
Write it on the line.

| job | jog | jet |

9. I help dogs and cats. It is my __job__ .

10. Look up! I am in a __jet__ .

Home Activity This page practices words that have the *j* sound heard in *just*. Work through the items with your child. Then with your child, search for things around your home that begin with the *j* sound, such as *jar*, *jelly*, *jug*, or *jeans*.

© Pearson Education A

Name_____

Say the word for each picture.
Circle the word.

wa<u>x</u>

---

1. 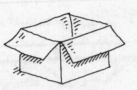 (box)

bend

2.  fat

(fox)

---

3.  sip

(six)

4. (ax)

at

---

5.  (mix)

map

6.  fist

(fix)

---

7.  ax

(ox)

8. 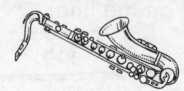 sad

(sax)

Find the word that has the same ending sound as .
Mark the ⬭ to show your answer.

9. ⬬ flex
   ⬭ flip
   ⬭ test

10. ⬭ dust
    ⬭ stand
    ⬬ tax

 Home Activity This page practices words that have the *x* sound heard in *wax*. Name each picture. Work through the items with your child. Then help your child make up a story about a fox in a box.

38 Phonics Xx/ks/

Practice Book Unit 2

© Pearson Education A

Name_____

Pick a word from the box to finish each sentence.
Write it on the line.

one   two   three

1. Ann has __two__ pals.

2. They have __three__ pets.

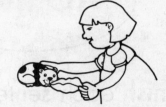

3. The best __one__ is Spot.

4. Spot likes to sit in __one__ big box.

5. Spot has __two__ pals just like Ann.

 Home Activity This page helps your child learn to read and write the words *one*, *two*, and *three*. Work through the items with your child. Then help your child write *one*, *two*, *three*, *1*, *2*, and *3* on separate index cards. Have him or her match the number words with the numerals.

© Pearson Education A

Name_____

Write the name of something you can share with your friends in each circle.

Possible answers:

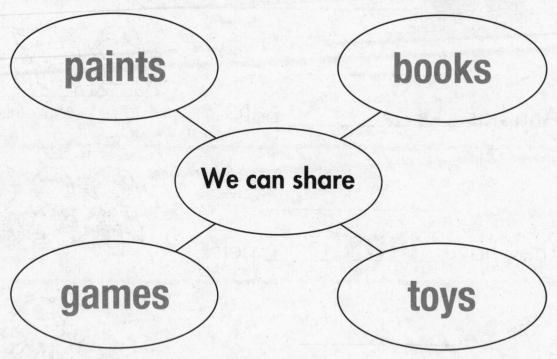

paints

books

We can share

games

toys

Finish each sentence. The words in the web may help you. **Write** the words on the lines.

1. We can share __paints__ .

2. We can share __games__ .

School + Home **Home Activity** This page helps your child finish sentences and learn to write sentences. Help your child write the sentences. Then have your child tell you some things he or she shares with friends.

40 **Writing**

Practice Book Unit 2

Name_____

Say the word for each picture.
Circle the picture if the word begins
with the **v** sound heard in **van**.

<u>v</u>an

1.

2.

3.

4.

5.

6.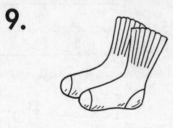

7.

8.

9.

10.

11.

12.

© Pearson Education A

School + Home

Home Activity This page practices words that have the *v* sound heard in *valley*. Work through the items with your child. Then have your child use the word for each circled picture above in a sentence.

Name_____

Say the word for each picture.
Circle the word to finish each sentence.
Write it on the line.

zebra

(buzz)   bust
_____

1. Bugs like to ___**buzz**___ .

jump   (jazz)
_____

2. The disk is ___**jazz**___ .

(zip)   zap
_____

3. I can ___**zip**___ up my vest.

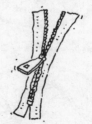

flop   (fuzz)
_____

4. Puff has soft ___**fuzz**___ .

(fizz)   fit
_____

5. Can you see the ___**fizz**___ ?

School + Home **Home Activity** This page practices words that have the z sound heard in zoo. Work through the items with your child. Then ask your child to tell you two words that start with the z sound and two words that end with the z sound.

Name_____

Pick a word from the box to match each picture.
Write it on the line.

> yam   yell   yak   yes   yo-yo   yap   yank   you

1.

you

2.

yo-yo

3.

yell

4.

yap

5.

yes

6.

yak

7.

yank

8.

yam

Find the word that has the **y** sound heard in .
Mark the ⬭ to show your answer.

9. ⬤ yet
   ⬭ went
   ⬭ van

10. ⬭ pest
   ⬤ yelp
   ⬭ men

 Home Activity This page practices words that have the y sound heard in *year*. Work through the items with your child. Ask your child to tell you the beginning sound in *yellow*. Then have him or her point out yellow objects in your home or neighborhood.

Name_____

Pick a word from the box to finish each sentence.
Write it on the line.

from	me	said

1. Brett is __**from**__ my ball club.

2. He helps __**me**__ hit the ball.

3. My vet Nan is __**from**__ here.

4. Nan __**said**__ she will help Kit.

5. Kit can help __**me**__ !

© Pearson Education A

Home Activity This page helps your child learn to read and write the words *from*, *me*, and *said*. Work through the items with your child. Then help your child write the words on index cards and practice reading them.

Name_____

Finish each sentence.
Write the words on the lines.

Possible answers:

1. Here is the __man__ .

2. He helps __pets__ .

3. Here is __Kim__ .

4. She helps __her friends__ .

Finish the sentence.
Tell something you do to help.

5. I help __walk dogs__ .

Home Activity This page helps your child finish sentences and learn to write sentences. Help your child write the sentences. Then talk with your child about what your family can do to be good neighbors. Write a list and put it on the refrigerator.

Name_____

Pick a word from the box to finish each sentence.
Write it on the line.

> quiz   quilt   quiet   quit

1. Fuzz and Puff are on the __quilt__ .

2. Little Dan is __quiet__ in his crib.

3. Tag must __quit__ !

4. Jill has a __quiz__ in class.

Animals talk in different ways. **Say** the word for the sound each animal makes. **Circle** the animal whose sound begins with the *q* sound heard in 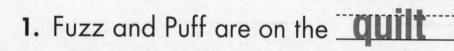 .

5.

© Pearson Education A

School + Home   **Home Activity** This page practices words that have the *q* sound heard in *quick*. Work through the items with your child. Then have your child read the words in the box and use each word in a spoken sentence.

Name_____

Say the word for each picture.
Circle the word.

du<u>ck</u>

---

1.  list
   (lick)

2.  clip
   (clock)

---

3. 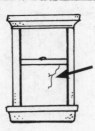 (crack)
   crab

4. past
   (pack)

---

5. 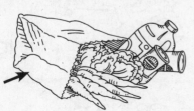 stamp
   (sack)

6.  (back)
   bad

---

7.  (stick)
   stand

8. jab
   (jack)

---

9.  task
   (tack)

10.  (sock)
    stop

 Home Activity This page practices words that end with the sound heard in *rack*. Name each picture and work through the items with your child. Then work together to make up silly sentences about ducks using words ending with *ck*, such as: *The duck wore a pack on his back.*

© Pearson Education A

Name_____

Say the word for each picture.
Circle the word.

pig<u>s</u>

1.  hat
(hats)

2. (lamp)
lamps

3.  bug
(bugs)

4.  duck
(ducks)

5.  cup
(cups)

6.  (lock)
locks

7.  (sled)
sleds

8. ant
(ants)

Find the word that means more than one.
Mark the ⬭ to show your answer.

9. ⬭ dress
   ⬭ gas
   ⬬ pins

10. ⬭ is
    ⬬ kids
    ⬭ has

 Home Activity This page practices words that end with -s and mean more than one. Work through the items with your child. Help your child name things in your home of which you have more than one, such as *shirts*, *socks*, *pets*, *chairs*, and *apples*. Emphasize the -s ending.

© Pearson Education A

Name_____

Pick a word from the box to finish each sentence.
Write it on the line.

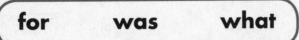

| for | was | what |

1. The cub __**was**__ little.

2. They can look __**for**__ fish in the pond.

3. Here is __**what**__ Mom can do.

4. Here is __**what**__ Dad can do.

5. They can run just __**for**__ fun!

Home Activity This page helps your child learn to read and write the words *for, was,* and *what.*
Work through the items with your child. Then take turns with your child finishing these sentences:
What can I do for …? I can …

Practice Book Unit 2   **High-Frequency Words** **49**

© Pearson Education A

Name_____

Look at the pictures. **Finish** each sentence.
Write the words on the lines.

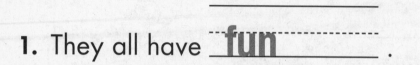

Possible answers:

1. They all have __**fun**__ .

2. They all have __**teeth**__ .

3. They all can __**play**__ .

4. They all can __**eat**__ .

5. **Draw** a picture of your family working together.

Pictures will vary.

© Pearson Education A

School + Home **Home Activity** This page helps your child finish sentences and learn to write sentences. Help your child write the sentences. Then ask your child the things your family may have in common with animal families, such as: *We play together. We eat together.*

Name_____

Add -s to each word.
Write the new word on the line.

1. hop **hops**   2. nap **naps**

3. get **gets**   4. see **sees**   5. help **helps**

Use the words you wrote to finish the sentences.
Write the words on the lines.

6. The bug **sees** a big plant.

7. The bug **hops** up the stem.

8. He **naps** on top in the sun.

9. The bug **gets** wet.

10. The plant **helps** the wet bug.

© Pearson Education A

Home Activity This page practices action words that end with -s, such as *jogs*. Work through the items with your child. Help your child think of different action words, such as *runs, hops, skips,* and *jumps,* and then have him or her act out each word.

Name_____

Add -ing to each word.
Write the new word on the line.

1. look <u>looking</u>   2. snack <u>snacking</u>

3. do <u>doing</u>   4. go <u>going</u>   5. jump <u>jumping</u>

Use the words you wrote to finish the sentences.
Write the words on the lines.

6. What is Pig <u>**doing**</u> ?

7. Pig is <u>**jumping**</u> in the plants!

8. Pig is <u>**snacking**</u> on my plants!

9. He is <u>**looking**</u> at the bugs.

10. Pig is <u>**going**</u> back in his pen!

 Home Activity This page practices words that end with -ing, such as *helping*. Work through the items with your child. Help your child write *look, jump, go, do,* and -ing on index cards. Then have him or her add -ing to each action word and read it aloud.

© Pearson Education A

Name_____

Circle a word to finish each sentence.
Write it on the line.

1. The sun is **yellow** .

_____

glass   green

2. My cat likes **green** grass.

_____

green   grab

3. The skunk sits next to a **green** plant.

_____

yet   yellow

4. He snacks on a **yellow** cob.

_____

blue   belt

5. The pup snacks on a **blue** sock.
Bad pup!

 School + Home
Home Activity This page helps your child learn to read and write the words *blue*, *green*, and *yellow*. Work through the items with your child. Then have your child point out objects that are blue, green, and yellow.

Name_____

Finish each sentence.
Write the words on the lines.

Possible answers:

1. Plants help  get **shade** .

2. Plants help  get **food** .

3. Plants help  get **water** .

4. Plants help  get **food** .

5. Plants help  and

get **food** .

Home Activity This page helps your child finish sentences and learn to write sentences. Help your child write the sentences. Then ask your child to tell you ways plants help people, such as: *Plants give people food.*

Name_____

Pick a word from the box to match each picture.
Write it on the line.

| net | frog | pup | mitt | spot | hill |
| flag | bell | tag | buzz | bed | drip |

1. flag

2. mitt

3. bell

4. frog

5. tag

6. pup

7. hill

8. drip

9. buzz

10. spot

11. bed

12. net

Home Activity This page practices words that have consonant and vowel letter patterns, such as *pet, stop,* and *well.* Name each picture. Work through the items with your child. Then help your child think of words that rhyme with the words on this page.

Name_____

Pick a word to finish each sentence. **Write** it on the line.

What   Where
_____

1. __**Where**__ is my hot dog?

Come   Clip
_____

2. __**Come**__ here and see!

pot   put
_____

3. Buzz __**put**__ a little bug on her lap.

was   where
_____

4. Here is __**where**__ she has a nap.

come   crab
_____

5. Ants __**come**__ to get a snack.

pit   put
_____

6. They will __**put**__ it on his back.

 School + Home **Home Activity** This page helps your child learn to read and write the words *come, put,* and *where.* Work through the items with your child. Then have him or her ask questions beginning with the word *where.*

© Pearson Education A

Name_____

Think of ways kids can help.
Think of ways bugs can help.
Write the words in the chart.

Kids can	Bugs can
help	eat
clean	help
eat	

Words in chart will vary. Possible answers:

Use words from the chart to finish the sentences.
Write the words on the lines.

1. Kids can _help_ .

2. Kids can _clean a mess_ .

3. Bugs can _help_ .

4. Bugs can _eat_ .

Home Activity This page helps your child learn to finish sentences. Help your child write the sentences. Have your child act out things he or she can do around the house. Have your child say what he or she is doing, such as: *I can set the table.*

© Pearson Education A

Name_____

Circle the correct word for each picture.

<u>sh</u>ed

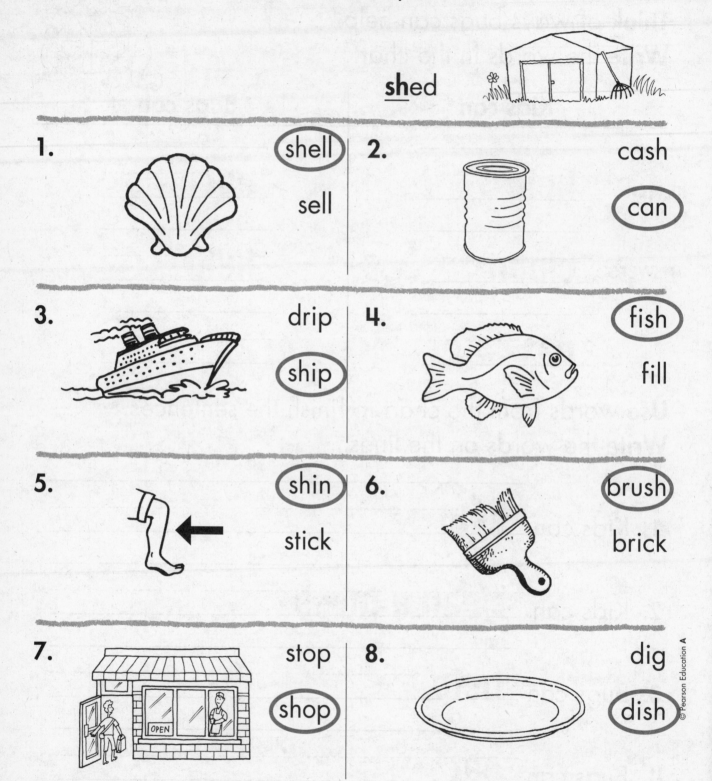

1. (shell)
   sell

2. cash
   (can)

3. drip
   (ship)

4. (fish)
   fill

5. (shin)
   stick

6. (brush)
   brick

7. stop
   (shop)

8. dig
   (dish)

Home Activity This page practices words with the *sh* sound. Work through the items with your child. Then help your child write these words and tell what they mean: *dish, shin, shell,* and *brush.*

Name_____

Read the word.
Circle the correct picture
for each word.   **th**ey

---

1. thick

2. bath

3. thin

4. three

5. cloth

6. path

Find the word that has the same beginning sound as .
Mark the ⬭ to show your answer.

7. ◯ pick
   ⬤ thick
   ◯ sick

8. ◯ bank
   ◯ tank
   ⬤ thank

Home Activity This page practices words with the *th* sound. Work through the items with your child. Then have your child write these words and tell what they mean: *thump, math,* and *cloth.*

© Pearson Education A

Name_____

Circle a word to finish each sentence.
Write it on the line.

b**all**

call   cat

_____

1. We ___**call**___ the dogs.

_____

wax   walk

_____

2. The dogs ___**walk**___ to us.

_____

all   add

_____

3. We ___**all**___ pet the dogs.

_____

talk   tack

_____

4. Mom can ___**talk**___ to the dogs.

_____

bell   ball

_____

5. The dogs see a ___**ball**___ .

Home Activity This page practices words with the *a* sound that is heard in *ball* and *talk*. Work through the items with your child. Help your child write these words that rhyme: *all, ball, call, fall, hall, tall,* and *wall.*

60 **Phonics** Vowel Sound in *ball*

Practice Book Unit 3

© Pearson Education A

Name_____

Look at the picture. **Circle** the answer to each question.
Hint: One question will have
two answers.

1. What has a hat?   the dog   (the cat)

2. What has a ball?   (the dog)   the cat

3. What has legs?   (the dog)   (the cat)

4. What is big?   the dog   (the cat)

5. What is little?   (the dog)   the cat

Nat   Deb   Pat

6. Which two dogs are the same?

_____   _____

Nat   **Pat**

7. Which dog is not like the others?

_____

Deb

School + Home   **Home Activity** This page helps your child identify how animal characters are alike and different. Work through the items with your child. Then ask your child to tell how the dog Deb is different from Nat and Pat.

© Pearson Education A

Name_____

Pick a word from the box to finish each sentence.
Write it on the line.

her	now	use

1. The man can __**use**__ the pen.

2. He is __**her**__ dad.

3. They will go __**now**__ .

4. He can see __**her**__ .

5. Come here __**now**__ .

Home Activity This page helps your child learn to read and write the words *her*, *now*, and *use*. Work through the items with your child. For practice, have your child look at each word in the box, read it, and spell it.

Name_____

Finish each sentence. **Write** the words on the lines. The words in the box may help you.

get big	too small	lots of shops
grow	in a city	

Possible answers are shown.

1. The pet shop is ___too small, in a city___ .

2. The shop can ___grow, get big___ .

3. A city has ___lots of shops___ .

4. Now the city can ___grow, get big___ .

5. Write a sentence about how places change.

___Sentences should tell how places change.___

___Example: A shop can get big.___

Home Activity This page helps your child finish sentences and learn to write sentences. Help your child write the sentences. Then read them together.

© Pearson Education A

Name_____

Say the word for each picture.
Circle the picture if the word
has the long **a** sound you
hear in **plane**.

pl**a**ne

---

1.  2.  3.

---

4.  5.  6.

---

7.  8.  9.

Circle the word to finish the sentence.
Write it on the line.

map   (skate)

_____

10. Ben likes to ___**skate**___ .

 Home Activity This page practices words with the long *a* sound. Work through the items with your child.
Help your child list two or three words that rhyme with *skate* and *wave*.

© Pearson Education A

Name_____

Say the word for each picture.
Write c on the line if you hear the
c sound as in **lace**.

la<u>c</u>e

1.

___ **c** ___ ent

2.

ra ___ **c** ___ e

3.

du _____

4.

___ **c** ___ ity

5.

la ___ ___ e

6.

fa ___ **c** ___ e

Find the word that has the same
sound as **c** in **city**.
Mark the ⬭ to show your answer.

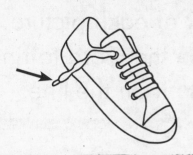

7. ⬭ tack
   ⬬ cell
   ⬭ bake

8. ⬭ can
   ⬭ hop
   ⬬ lace

Home Activity This page practices words with the c sound heard in *race*. Work through the items with your child. Then have your child write these words and tell what they mean: *place, space, lace.*

Name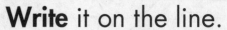_____

Look at each picture.
Circle the word to finish each sentence.
Write it on the line.

gem

(age)   wag   nap
_____

1. Lin's _____**age**_____ is six.

egg   gap   (stage)
_____

2. She can sing on the _____**stage**_____ .

cap   (cage)   gate
_____

3. Jon can see a _____**cage**_____ .

hall   (gem)   dog
_____

4. He can see a _____**gem**_____ .

(page)   grape   pan
_____

5. Lin and Jon read the _____**page**_____ .

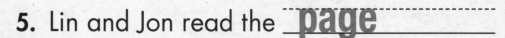

 Home Activity This page practices words with the *g* sound heard in *rage*. Work through the items with your child. Help your child write these words and use each in a sentence: *stage*, *age*, and *page*.

66 **Phonics** *g/j/*   **Practice Book Unit 3**

© Pearson Education A

Name_____

Look at the pictures.
Circle the answer to each question.

Kate

Shane

1. Who has a pet? Kate (Shane)

2. Who can read? Kate (Shane)

3. Who is with her mom? (Kate) Shane

4. Who gets help? (Kate) Shane

5. Who is little? (Kate) Shane

6. Who sits by a gate? Kate (Shane)

7. Draw two faces that are the same.
Children should draw two similar faces.

8. Draw two faces that are different.
Children should draw two different faces.

School + Home **Home Activity** This page helps your child identify how two people are different. Work through the items with your child. Then ask your child to show different faces that people can make, like happy or sad faces.

Name_____

Pick a word from the box to finish each sentence.
Write it on the line.

old	too	want

_____
1. Jen and Kim __**want**__ to skate.

_____
2. Tad can skate __**too**__ .

_____
3. They __**want**__ to help Tad.

_____
4. Jen has __**old**__ skates.

_____
5. Pup wants to play __**too**__ .

School + Home

Home Activity This page helps your child learn to read and write the words *old*, *too*, and *want*. Work through the items with your child. Help your child make up a story about the snow using these words.

Name_____

Finish each sentence. **Write** the words on the lines.
The words in the box may help you.

smile	**spell**	**get help**
hit a ball	**make a mess**	**run a race**

Possible answers are shown.

1. A baby can not __spell, hit a ball, run a race__ .

2. A baby can __smile, make a mess, cry__ .

3. I can __spell, hit a ball, run a race__ .

4. A baby and I can __smile, get help, sleep__ .

5. **Write** a sentence about what you can do now that you are big. Write your sentence on the lines.

_____

__Sentences should tell things children can do.__

_____

__Example: I can play a game.__

Home Activity This page helps your child finish sentences and learn to write sentences. Help your child write the sentences. Then help your child think of more things he or she can do now.

Name

Circle the word for each picture.

m<u>i</u>ce

1. (five) face

2. 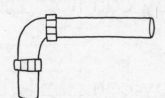 back (bike)

3.  dim (dime)

4. 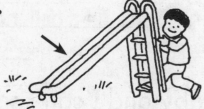 (pipe) pin

5.  (kite) kick

6. 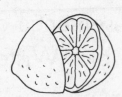 slip (slide)

7. (smile) snake

8.  (lime) lid

9.  vase (vine)

10. (hive) had

Home Activity This page practices words with the long *i* sound. Work through the items with your child. Help your child make flashcards of some long *i* words. Have your child practice reading the words.

Name_____

Read the word.
Circle the correct picture for
each word.

whisk

---

1. whale

2. whip

Circle a word to finish each sentence.
Write it on the line.

(When)   They

3. ___When___ can we go?

talk   (whack)

4. Tim can ___whack___ the ball.

Find the word that has the same sound as **wh** in **when.**
Mark the ⬭ to show your answer.

5. ⬛ whiff
⬭ shine
⬭ that

6. ⬭ fish
⬭ hole
⬛ whack

 School + Home **Home Activity** This page practices words with the *wh* sound heard in *while.* Work through the items with your child. Then have your child write these words and use each in a sentence: *whale, when, while.*

© Pearson Education A

Name_____

Read the word.
Circle the picture
for each word.

check  wa**tch**

---

1. catch

2. chest

---

3. patch

4. chin

---

5. match

6. chop

Find the word that has the same sound as **ch** in **much**.
Mark the ⬯ to show your answer.

7. ⬯ wake
　　 ⬬ ditch
　　 ⬯ ship

8. ⬯ city
　　 ⬬ chill
　　 ⬯ cape

 Home Activity This page practices words with the *ch* sound heard in *pitch*. Work through the items with your child. Help your child write these words and practice reading them aloud: *chip, pitch, chill, chick, watch, itch, rich, chase.*

72 Phonics Digraphs *ch, tch*　　　　**Practice Book Unit 3**

Name_____

Look at the pictures.
Circle the answer to
each question.
Hint: One question will
have two answers.

Ana   Mike

1. Who will pitch?   Ana   (Mike)

2. Who has a bike?   (Ana)   Mike

3. Who has a ball?   Ana   (Mike)

4. Who has stripes?   Ana   (Mike)

5. Who rides the bike?   (Ana)   Mike

6. Who can have fun?   (Ana)   (Mike)

7. Write one way that Ana and Mike are the same.

_____

Sample answer: Ana and Mike can smile.

8. Write one way that Ana and Mike are not the same.

_____

Sample answer: She is a girl. He is a boy.

 School +Home **Home Activity** This page helps your child identify how two characters are the same and different. Work through the items with your child. Then have your child tell more ways that the characters are the same or different.

Name_____

Pick a word from the box to finish each sentence.
Write it on the line.

| there who your |

1. __**Who**__ will go on the trip?

2. The bus is here for __**your**__ trip.

3. The pet shop is __**there**__ .

4. This is the man __**who**__ helps the pets.

5. The dogs are __**there**__ .

© Pearson Education A

Name_____

Finish each sentence. **Write** the words on the lines. The words in the box may help you.

chat	**walk**	**get big**	**stand up**
smile	**swim**	**stack blocks**	**snap up bugs**

Possible answers are shown.

1. A duck can __walk, get big, swim, snap up bugs, stand up__ .

2. I can __chat, walk, smile, stand up__ .

3. I can __get big, swim, stack blocks__ .

4. A duck and I can __walk, get big, swim, stand up__ .

5. Write a sentence about what ducks can do.

__Sentences should tell things ducks can do.__

__Example: Ducks can swim in a lake.__

School + Home **Home Activity** This page helps your child finish sentences and learn to write sentences. Help your child write words in the sentences. Then discuss how living things can grow.

Name _____

Write a word from the box to match each picture.

bone	nose
rope	stone
robe	smoke
hose	note
rose	

c<u>o</u>ne

1.

_____

rope

2.

_____

rose

3.

_____

bone

4.

_____

robe

5.

_____

smoke

6.

_____

nose

7.

_____

note

8.

_____

hose

9.

_____

stone

© Pearson Education A

 School + Home

Home Activity This page practices words with the long *o* sound. Work through the items with your child. Then help your child make up a rhyme using the words *rose*, *nose*, and *those*.

Name_____

Read each sentence.
Circle the contraction for the underlined words.

I will come with you.   I'll come with you.

1. You will find the garden.   (You'll)   Hasn't

2. The bug was not here.   (wasn't)   didn't

3. I can not pick the bud.   aren't   (can't)

4. We will smell the rose.   (We'll)   Wasn't

5. The bugs are not big.   haven't   (aren't)

Home Activity This page practices contractions with *'ll* and *n't*. Work through the items with your child. Then say a contraction, such as *didn't*. Have your child tell the two words that were combined to make the contraction.

Practice Book Unit 3   **Contractions** *'ll* and *n't* **77**

Name_____

Write the contraction for each pair of words.

1. is not _**isn't**_

I am here for the game.
I'm here for the game.

2. had not _**hadn't**_

3. I am _**I'm**_

4. he will _**he'll**_

5. was not _**wasn't**_

6. they will _**they'll**_

7. I will _**I'll**_

8. did not _**didn't**_

Find the contraction.
Mark the ⬭ to show your answer.

9. ⬭ am
   ⬬ I'm
   ⬭ I am

10. ⬭ has
    ⬭ have
    ⬬ hasn't

Home Activity This page practices contractions with *'m, 'll,* and *n't,* such as *I'm, I'll,* and *can't.* Work through the items with your child. Then help your child write *he, she, I, you, we, am, not,* and *will* on index cards and make contractions.

Name_____

Look at the pictures.

Write 1, 2, 3 to put the sentences in order.

1. At last plants can grow. _____ **3** _____

2. The snow is cold. _____ **1** _____

3. The hot sun melts the snow. _____ **2** _____

4. The bug lands on the rose. _____ **2** _____

5. First there is a rose. _____ **1** _____

6. Then the bug takes a nap. _____ **3** _____

 Home Activity This page helps your child put events in order to form a story. Work through the items with your child. Then ask your child to draw a series of pictures showing three events in the order in which they happen.

Name_____

Pick a word from the box to finish each sentence.
Write it on the line.

> could   eat   very

1. The bug ___could___ fly.

2. This bug will ___eat___ the plant.

3. The wind is ___very___ cold.

4. The roses ___could___ go there.

5. Now the sun is ___very___ hot.

© Pearson Education A

Home Activity This page helps your child learn to read and write the words *could*, *eat*, and *very*. Work through the items with your child. Then have your child use each word in a sentence about how seasons change each year.

Name _____

Finish each sentence. **Write** the words on the lines.
The words in the box may help you. **Possible responses are shown.**

dig holes	pop up	get big	eat plants
help plants	can hide	kill plants	

1. The sun helps plants <u>pop up, get big</u> .

2. Some bugs <u>eat plants, can hide</u> .

3. Bad bugs <u>kill plants</u> .

Write two sentences about what you can do
in a garden. Write your sentences on the lines.

4. <u>Example: I can help plants.</u>
_____
_____
_____

5. <u>Example: I dig holes.</u>
_____
_____
_____

Home Activity This page helps your child finish sentences and learn to write sentences. Help your child write the sentences. Then have your child think up a story about bugs.

Practice Book Unit 3

© Pearson Education A

Name_____

Circle the correct word for each picture.

St**e**ve    m**u**le

---

1.    (cube)
cub

2.    tub
(tube)

---

3.    (duck)
duke

4.    pet
(Pete)

---

5. 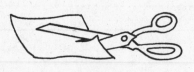   (cut)
cute

6.    (cub)
cube

---

7.    egg
(Eve)

8.    fluff
(flute)

 Home Activity This page practices words with the long *u* and long *e* sounds, as in *mule* and *Steve*. Work through the items with your child. Then say these words and names, and have your child find them on the page: *tube, Pete, cute, Eve,* and *mule.*

Name_____

Pick a word from the box
to match each picture.
Write it on the line.

b**ee**

feet   he   queen   she   sheep   tree

1.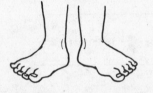
feet

2.
he

3.
sheep

4.
she

5.
queen

6.
tree

Find the word that has the same vowel sound as .
Mark the ⬭ to show your answer.

7. ⬛ me
   ⬭ met
   ⬭ mat

8. ⬭ wed
   ⬭ wad
   ⬛ weed

 Home Activity This page practices words with the long *e* sound spelled *e* or *ee*, as in *me* and *keep*. Work through the items with your child. Then have your child say a rhyming word for these words: *need, beep, peel, we,* and *sheet.*

© Pearson Education A

Name_____

Look at the pictures.
Write 1, 2, 3 to put the sentences in order.

1. Dan and Frank catch a fish. _____**3**_____

2. Dan and Frank sit by the lake. _____**1**_____

3. Dan feels a tug. _____**2**_____

4. Min puts on her skates. _____**2**_____

5. Min skates from place to place. _____**3**_____

6. Min gets two skates. _____**1**_____

 Home Activity This page helps your child put events in order to form a story. Work through the items with your child. Then have your child tell about something that happened at school. Ask what happened first, next, and last.

© Pearson Education A

Name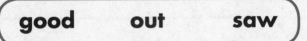

Pick a word from the box to finish each sentence.
Write it on the line.

good out saw

1. The dog ___**saw**___ Kent.

2. The dog went ___**out**___ to play.

3. Kent ___**saw**___ his dog in the grass.

4. Kent came ___**out**___ too.

5. Kent and his pet had a ___**good**___ time!

© Pearson Education A

School + Home **Home Activity** This page helps your child learn to read and write the words *good*, *out*, and *saw*. Work through the items with your child. Then have your child close his or her eyes and spell the words as you say them.

Name_____

Find words to finish each sentence. **Write** the words on the line. The words in the box may help you.

can	walk	has	swim	big
small	legs	is	see	

Accept reasonable answers.

1. A baby frog can <u>swim, see</u>_____.

2. A baby frog
gets big. The frog <u>has legs, can swim</u>.

3. A baby snake <u>is small, can see</u>.

4. A baby snake
gets big. The snake <u>is big, can see</u>.

5. A baby <u>has legs, is small</u>.

6. The baby gets
to be a kid. The kid <u>is big, can walk</u>.

© Pearson Education A

Home Activity This page gives practice in finishing sentences. Help your child write the sentences. Then read them together. Ask your child to name one way he or she has changed while growing.

Name_____

Pick a word from the box to finish each sentence.
Add **-ed** to each word. **Write** it on the line.

walk   play   look   help   dress

1. Al woke up and got __**dressed**__ .

2. He __**walked**__ to school with Jan.

3. Al __**looked**__ at two books.

4. He __**played**__ a game at lunch.

5. Al __**helped**__ Lee with math.

© Pearson Education A

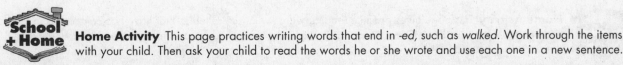

School + Home

Home Activity This page practices writing words that end in *-ed,* such as *walked.* Work through the items with your child. Then ask your child to read the words he or she wrote and use each one in a new sentence.

Name_____

Circle the word for each picture.

ra**bb**it

1.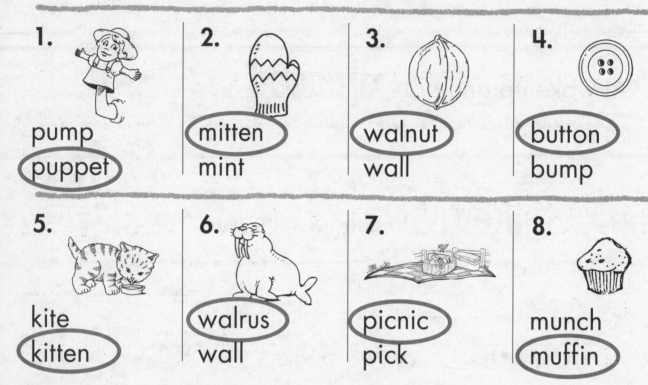

pump
(puppet)

2. mitten
mint

3. walnut
wall

4. button
bump

---

5. kite
(kitten)

6. (walrus)
wall

7. (picnic)
pick

8. munch
(muffin)

Write the word for each picture.

9.

basket
base

10.

hello
helmet

basket

helmet

© Pearson Education A

 School + Home **Home Activity** This page gives practice reading words with two syllables that have two consonants in the middle. Work through the items with your child. Then have your child choose three of the circled words and use each in a sentence.

Practice Book Unit 3

Name_____

Write 1, 2, 3 in each row to show the right order.

1. | **2**

2. | **1**

3. | **3**

4. | **3**
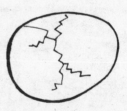

5. | **2**

6. | **1**

Draw a picture to show what happens next.
Write a sentence about your picture.

7.

Child should draw
a picture of a baby
bird here.

Sentences should tell about a chick or baby bird hatching

from an egg.

School + Home **Home Activity** This page gives your child practice putting pictures in order to form a story. Have your child choose one of the scenes from above. Then help your child write sentences that tell what happened first, next, and last in the story.

Name_____

Pick a word from the box to finish each sentence.
Write it on the line.

down   way   work

1. Here is the ___way___ to the pond.

2. We must go ___down___ the hill.

3. We see a man at ___work___ .

4. This is the ___way___ to skate.

5. I do not like to fall ___down___ .

© Pearson Education A

Name_____

Write an answer to each question.
The words in the box may help you.

Possible answers are shown.

green buds	kids with rakes	school bus	sun
kids on bikes	tall grass	roses	ice
kids in hats	kids swim	bugs	

1. What can you see in spring?

   I can see __green buds, bugs, kids on bikes__.

2. What can you see in summer?

   I can see __tall grass, sun, kids swim, roses__.

3. What can you see in fall?

   I can see __kids with rakes, a school bus__.

4. What can you see in winter?

   I can see __ice, kids in hats__.

5. What is the best time of year?

   _____

   I think __Sentence should tell about the child's favorite season.__.

Home Activity This page gives practice in writing sentences to answer questions. Help your child write the sentences. Then read them together. Ask your child to name three things that can be seen during his or her favorite season.

Circle a word to finish each sentence.
Write it on the line.

fly

(my)   met

_____

1. I walk with __my_____ cat.

---

be   (by)

_____

2. We sit __by_____ a tree.

---

skip   (sky)

_____

3. We look up at the __sky_____.

(try)   tap

_____

4. We will __try_____ to run fast.

(dry)   drip

_____

5. We like to be __dry_____.

 Home Activity This page practices words with the long *i* sound of *y*, as in *fly* or *try*. Work through the items with your child. Then talk about these words and help your child write them: *fry, cry, shy,* and *spy.*

Name_____

Circle the correct word for each picture.

penny

1.  (**puppy**)

   put

2.  jeep

   (**jelly**)

3.  sum

   (**sunny**)

4. 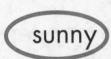 (**happy**)

   hatch

5. **20** (**twenty**)

   try

6.  (**mommy**)

   mitten

7.  bump

   (**bunny**)

8.  must

   (**muddy**)

Find the word that has the same **y** sound as candy.
Mark the ⬭ to show your answer.

9. ⬭ say
   ⬮ silly
   ⬭ smile

10. ⬮ funny
    ⬭ fresh
    ⬭ fly

 School + Home **Home Activity** This page practices words with the long *e* sound of *y*, as in *bumpy* and *sandy*. Work through the items with your child. Then challenge your child to choose three words he or she circled and use them in sentences.

Name_____

Read each story.

Circle the sentence that tells what the story is all about.

Then **circle** the picture that tells what the story is about.

1. Jill helps Mom.

She picks up socks.

She takes them to Mom.

She sweeps up.

2.

3. Ben sees a cat.

He sees a puppy.

Then he sees a fish.

Ben can see the pets.

4.

Read the story. **Write** a title for this story.

_____

5. _Accept reasonable titles, such as Fun at Camp._

Holly has fun at camp.

She can go on hikes.

She can swim in a lake.

She can sleep in a tent too.

© Pearson Education A

Home Activity This page helps your child identify main ideas of stories. Work through the items with your child. Then ask your child to make up titles for the first two little stories on this page.

Name_____

Circle a word to finish each sentence.
Write it on the line.

them   (their)

1. Ned and Pam see _____**their**_____ dad.

how   (some)

2. Dad has a can and _____**some**_____ rags.

(how)   have

3. The kids see _____**how**_____ Dad works.

of   (other)

4. The kids pick up the _____**other**_____ rags.

(their)   how

5. Ned and Pam help _____**their**_____ dad.

© Pearson Education A

 Home Activity This page helps your child learn to read and write the words *how, other, some,* and *their.* Write *How do you help at home?* on a sheet of paper. Help your child read the question aloud and write an answer in a sentence.

Name_____

Finish the sentences. **Write** the words on the lines.
The words in the box may help you.

| do well at school | | help them |
| get a gift | make my bed | go on a trip |

Possible answers
are shown.

I can do a nice thing for my mom or dad.

1. I can <u>do well at school</u> .

2. I can <u>help them</u> .

3. I can <u>make my bed</u> .

I can have a good time too!

4. I can <u>get a gift</u> .

5. I can <u>go on a trip</u> .

Home Activity This page gives practice in finishing sentences. Help your child write the sentences. Then read them together. Ask your child to describe a surprise that he or she has given or received.

© Pearson Education A

Name_____

Circle the word for each picture.

ki**ng**

si**nk**

---

1. (bank) bent

2. sing (swing)

3. truck (tank)

4. (skunk) skate

---

5. rink (ring)

6. bunk (band)

7. wind (wing)

8. (sing) slip

Find the word that has the same ending sound as .
Mark the ⬭ to show your answer.

9. ⬛ pink
⬭ pick
⬭ pile

10. ⬭ gum
⬭ jacks
⬛ junk

 School + Home **Home Activity** This page practices words that end with *ng* and *nk*. Work through the items with your child. Then ask your child to make a list of words that rhyme with *wink*, *sank*, and *thing*.

Name_____

Say the word for each picture.
Write nk on the line if the word has the same ending sound as **pink**.
Write ng on the line if the word has the same ending sound as **sting**.

pi**nk**

sti**ng**

1.

sti **nk** _____

2.

sku **nk** _____

3.

spri **ng** _____

4.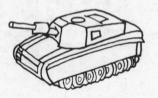

ta **nk** _____

5.

ca _____

6.

stri **ng** _____

7.

ni _____

8.

i **nk** _____

9.

wi **nk** _____

© Pearson Education A

 Home Activity This page practices words that end with *ing*, *ink*, *ank*, and *unk*. Work through the items with your child. Then have your child write the following words and use each in a sentence: *think*, *thank*, *junk*, and *bring*.

Name_____

Read the story.

Circle the sentence that tells what the story is all about.

Then **circle** the picture that shows what the story is all about.

1. ⟨Jane looks happy.⟩
She makes a glad face.
She smiles.
She grins.

2.

3. Teddy walks the dog.
⟨Teddy likes his dog.⟩
He pets the dog.
Teddy hugs the dog.

4.

5. Shan cut some shapes.
She stuck them on the shade.
She put on some dots.
⟨Shan made a lamp look nice.⟩

6.

Home Activity This page helps your child identify the main idea in a story. Work through the items with your child. Then read one of your child's favorite stories. Ask him or her to tell you what the story is all about.

Name_____

Pick a word from the box to finish each sentence.
Write it on the line.

any	friend	new	our

1. This is **our** cat Skip.

2. We will make Skip a **new** home.

3. My **friend** Kate is here too.

4. We don't need **any** help at all.

5. Skip has made a new **friend** !

© Pearson Education A

Home Activity This page helps your child learn to read and write the words *any, friend, new,* and *our.* Work through the items with your child. Help your child write these words on cards and practice reading them aloud.

Name_____

Think of your favorite books. **Finish** each sentence.
Write the words on the lines.
The words in the box may help you.

make snacks	get games
smile	sad
happy	sing songs
try new things	see new places

Possible answers are shown.

1. I like to _make snacks, try new things, see new places, sing songs_

2. Books can help us _try new things, make snacks, see new places_

3. Books can help us _sing songs, get games, smile_

4. Books can make me feel _happy, sad_

5. Write a sentence about what books can help you do.

Sentences should tell what books can do.

Example: Books can help me see new places.

Home Activity This page helps your child finish sentences and learn to write a sentence. Your child can use words from the box or other words. Help your child finish the sentences. Then talk about your child's favorite books or stories.

© Pearson Education A

Pick a word from the box to finish each compound word.
Write it on the line.
Draw a line to the picture it matches.

pancake

ball   box   cake   pack

1. base **ball** _____

2. cup **cake** _____

3. back **pack** _____

4. sand **box** _____

5.

6.

7.

8.

Find the compound word.
Mark the ⬭ to show your answer.

9. ⬬ bedtime
   ⬭ picnic
   ⬭ kitten

10. ⬭ in
    ⬬ inside
    ⬭ sides

Home Activity This page provides practice recognizing compound words. Work through the items with your child. Then help your child find things with names that are compound words, such as: *toothbrush*, *bathtub*, and *flashlight*.

Name_____

Say the word for each picture.
Write es if the picture shows
more than one.

box**es**

1.

dish **es**

2.

ax **es**

3.

bus **es**

4.

glass **es**

5.

dress **es**

6.

bench ____

7.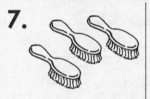

brush **es**

8.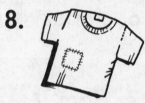

patch ____

Pick a word from the box to finish each sentence.
Write it on the line.

> inches   foxes

9. I saw two cute __foxes__ .

10. One of them was 20 __inches__ long.

School + Home **Home Activity** This page helps your child add -es to nouns to make them mean more than one. Work through the items with your child. Then have your child choose three of the words with -es at the end and use them in one sentence.

© Pearson Education A

Name_____

Add -es to each word.
Write the new word on the line.

_____
1. buzz _buzzes_ | **2.** munch _munches_

_____
3. rush _rushes_ | **4.** mix _mixes_ | **5.** pass _passes_

Use the words you wrote to finish the sentences.
Write the words on the lines.

6. A bee **buzzes** , and Sam runs.

7. Sam **rushes** to see Ming.

8. Ming **mixes** fun snacks on a dish.

9. Ming **passes** the dish to Sam.

10. Sam **munches** one of the snacks.

© Pearson Education A

![School + Home logo] **Home Activity** This page helps your child practice adding *-es* to verbs. Work through the items with your child. Then have your child add *-es* to the following verbs and act out the actions: *mix, wax,* and *catch.*

Name_____

Read the story.
Circle the sentence that tells what the story is all about.
Then **write** a title for the story.

Possible titles are shown.

1. Tess has one dog.
   She has two cats.
   She has three fish.
   (Tess has lots of pets.)

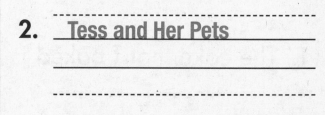

2. ___Tess and Her Pets___

3. (Ruff likes to rest.)
   He sits in the hall.
   Ruff sleeps on the rug.
   He rests on the grass.

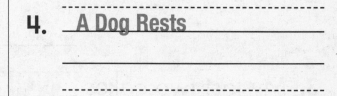

4. ___A Dog Rests___

5. (We will go on a trip.)
   We will pack.
   We will take a cab.
   We will go on a plane.

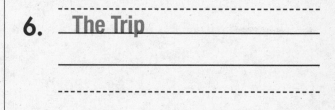

6. ___The Trip___

School + Home **Home Activity** This page helps your child identify the main idea of a story. Work through the items with your child. Then look at the stories together again. Ask your child to tell about each story in his or her own words.

Name_____

Pick a word from the box to finish each sentence.
Write it on the line.

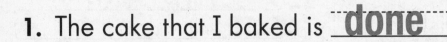

| again | done | know | were |

1. The cake that I baked is __done__ .

2. We __know__ that it is big.

3. My last two cakes __were__ not this big.

4. Now will you make a cake __again__ ?

5. We like it when a cake is __done__ .

 Home Activity This page helps your child learn to read and write the words *again*, *done*, *know*, and *were*. Work through the items with your child. Say the words one at a time. Ask your child to use each word in a sentence.

© Pearson Education A

Name_____

Finish each sentence. The words in the box may help you.

big lakes	hike	take trips	cliffs
tall trees	caves	ride on ships	see a city

Possible answers are shown.

1. I can see ___big lakes, tall trees, caves, cliffs___ in the U.S.A.

2. I can ___take trips, see a city, hike, ride on ships___ in the U.S.A.

3. I want to see ___big lakes, caves, cliffs, tall trees___ in the U.S.A.

Write two sentences about what you want to do in the U.S.A.

4. ___Example: I want to ride on ships.___

_____

_____

5. ___Example: I want to hike.___

_____

_____

School + Home

Home Activity This page gives practice in finishing and writing sentences about places. Help your child write the sentences. Read the sentences together. Then have your child draw a picture of one place he or she would like to visit in the U.S.A.

© Pearson Education A

Name_____

for**k**    st**ore**

Say the word for each picture. Circle the word.

1.    (corn)

cone

2.    (storm)

stone

3.    port

(pot)

4.   code

(core)

5.    home

(horn)

6.    (thorn)

toss

7.    (fort)

fog

8.    stock

(stork)

© Pearson Education A

 School + Home **Home Activity** This page practices words with the sound of *or* heard in *fork* and *ore* heard in *store*. Name each picture. Then say these words to your child: *sore, tack, cord, car, porch, star, mark, more.* Have your child stand if a word has an *or/ore* sound and sit if it does not.

Name_____

Say the word for each picture.
Circle the word.

f<u>ar</u>m

1.

(car)
core
cot

2.

jot
jab
(jar)

3.

yam
yak
(yarn)

4.

am
(arm)
on

5.

pan
(park)
port

6.

cab
(card)
cord

7.

(star)
stack
store

8.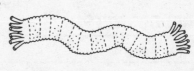

score
scope
(scarf)

9.

cord
cast
(cart)

10.

(shark)
short
shake

Home Activity This page practices words with the *ar* sound heard in *farm*. Name each picture and work through the items with your child. Then have your child tell you a short story about a visit to a farm. Encourage your child to use at least three words that have the *ar* sound.

© Pearson Education A

Name_____

Look at the picture. Circle the answer to each question. Hint: One question will have two answers.

Dad   Meg

1. Who has a rag?   (Meg)   Dad

2. Who has a hose?   Meg   (Dad)

3. Who has glasses?   (Meg)   (Dad)

4. Who has pants?   Meg   (Dad)

5. Who has a top with dots? (Meg)   Dad

6. Write one other way that Meg and her dad are the same.

   Possible answers:

   _____

   They have a cap. They have socks. They have two legs.

7. Write one other way that Meg and her dad are NOT the same.

   Possible answers:

   _____

   Dad is big. Meg is little. Meg has shorts.

Home Activity This page helps your child identify how two people are alike and different. Work through the items with your child. Then ask your child to name one way the two of you are alike and one way the two of you are different.

Name_____

Pick a word from the box to finish each sentence.
Write it on the line.

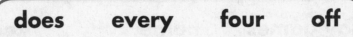

does   every   four   off

1. Rick **does** chores at home.

2. He sweeps the porch **every** day.

3. He uses a rag to wipe **off** marks.

4. There are **four** fish to feed, too.

5. Rick **does** a lot to help at home.

 Home Activity This page helps your child learn to read and write the words *does, every, four,* and *off.* Write each word on a card and lay the cards facedown. Have your child pick up each card, say the word, and use it in a sentence.

© Pearson Education A

Name_____

Think about a special place you enjoy.
Read the questions. **Finish** the sentences.

park	play games	home	zoo
shore	swim	see animals	look at books

Possible answers are shown.

1. What is your place?

_____

It is __the park, the zoo, the shore, home._____ .

2. What do you do in your place?

_____

I __play games, see animals, swim, look at books_____ .

3. **Draw** a picture of your place.

Pictures should show the special place that the child wrote about.

4. **Write** a sentence about your place.

Sentences should tell about the place the child drew.

_____

_____

_____

© Pearson Education A

 School + Home **Home Activity** This page helps your child practice writing sentences to describe a special place. Work with your child to write the sentences. Then read them together.

Practice Book Unit 4

h**er**   b**ir**d   c**ur**l

Say the word for each picture. **Circle** the word.

1.    (skirt)
   skit

2.    (girl)
   get

3.    (burn)
   barn

4.    fin
   (fern)

5.    dart
   (dirt)

6.    porch
   (perch)

7.    (shirt)
   sharp

8.    cluck
   (clerk)

Find the word that has the same middle sound as .
Mark the ⬭ to show your answer.

9. ▬ firm
   ⬭ form
   ⬭ farm

10. ⬭ tune
    ⬭ torn
    ▬ turn

 Home Activity This page practices words spelled with *er, ir,* and *ur* with the sound heard in the middle of *her, dirt,* and *turn.* Make up riddles about the pictures, such as: *I am green and I grow. What am I?* (fern) Have your child point to the correct picture and say its name.

Double the last letter in each word. **Add -ed** to each word. **Write** the new word on the line.

1. rip **ripped**   2. drop **dropped**

Double the last letter in each word. **Add -ing** to each word. **Write** the new word on the line.

3. shop **shopping**   4. grab **grabbing**

Use the words you wrote to finish the sentences. **Write** the words on the lines.

5. Mom and Sam are **shopping** .

6. Sam is **grabbing** a bag for Mom.

7. Sam **dropped** the bag.

8. The bag **ripped** and made a mess.

 Home Activity This page practices writing words that end in -ed and -ing, such as *planned* and *stopping*. Write the following words on a sheet of paper and have your child add -ed and -ing to each one: *clap, nod, hum.* Have your child act out each word.

© Pearson Education A

Name_____

Look at the pictures. **Write** to tell about the pets. **Use** the words in the box. **Hint:** You will use one set of words two times.

bird   fish

| has fins | has wings | in a tank | in a cage |
| must eat | has feet | can swim | |

The order may vary, but all phrases for **bird** 1–4 should relate to the bird.

1. <u>has wings</u>

_____

2. <u>in a cage</u>

_____

3. <u>must eat</u>

_____

4. <u>has feet</u>

The order may vary, but all phrases for **fish** 5–8 should relate to the fish.

5. <u>has fins</u>

_____

6. <u>in a tank</u>

_____

7. <u>must eat</u>

_____

8. <u>can swim</u>

© Pearson Education A

Home Activity This page helps your child identify how two animals are alike and different. Help your child name another way birds and fish are alike and different, such as: *Birds and fish have tails. Birds can fly but fish cannot fly.*

Name_____

Pick a word from the box to finish each sentence.
Write it on the line.

| about   family   once   together |

1. My ___**family**___ likes to ride bikes.

2. We ride our bikes ___**once**___ a week.

3. We sit ___**together**___ and rest.

4. It is ___**about**___ time to go.

5. It is fun to ride with my ___**family**___ !

 Home Activity This page helps your child learn to read and write the words *about*, *family*, *once*, and *together*. Point to the words in the box one at a time. Have your child say each word aloud and use it in a sentence.

© Pearson Education A

Name_____

Think about something you have that you like a lot.
Draw a picture of it in the box. **Read** the questions.
Finish the sentences on the lines. **Accept reasonable answers.**

1.

> Picture should show child's special object.

2. What is it?

It is <u>Answer should name the object.</u> .

3. What does it look like?

It is <u>Answer should describe what the object looks like.</u> .

4. Where did you get it?

I got it <u>Answer should tell where the child got the object.</u> .

5. What do you do with it?

I <u>Answer should tell what the child likes to do with the object.</u> .

© Pearson Education A

 Home Activity This page helps your child practice writing sentences to describe a special object he or she owns. Work with your child to write the sentences. Then read them together. If possible, let your child hold the object while reading.

Name_____

Write the contraction for each
pair of words.

He is tired.
He's tired.

1. she + is = <u>**she's**</u>

2. it + is = <u>**it's**</u>

3. here + is = <u>**here's**</u>

4. who + is = <u>**who's**</u>

5. that + is = <u>**that's**</u>

6. what + is = <u>**what's**</u>

Find the contraction.
Mark the ⬭ to show your answer.

7. ⬭ whats
   ⬮ he's
   ⬭ there

8. ⬮ that's
   ⬭ this
   ⬭ hats

Home Activity This page practices making contractions with *'s*, such as *here's*. Work through the items with
your child. Then ask your child to use the words *he's*, *she's*, and *it's* in sentences.

Name _____

Pick a word from the box that means the same as each pair of words. **Write** it on the line.

| you're | they've | I've |
| you've | they're | we've |

We are pals.
We're pals.

1. we + have =

   we've

2. you + are =

   you're

3. I + have =

   I've

4. you + have =

   you've

Look at each picture. **Write** the contraction to finish each sentence.

| They're | I've | They've |

5. **They're** in a box.

6. **I've** won a prize.

Home Activity This page practices making contractions with *'ve and 're*, such as *we've* and *they're*. Work through the items with your child. Then write *we, they, he, she, is, are,* and *have* on index cards and see how many contractions your child can make.

Practice Book Unit 4   **Phonics** Contractions *'ve* and *'re* **119**

© Pearson Education A

Name_____

Read the sentences in the story.
Write 1, 2, 3 to show the right order.

_____
1. __**3**__ Kim shares her grapes
with Lan.

_____
2. __**1**__ Kim has some grapes.

_____
3. __**2**__ Lan wants some grapes too.

Read the sentence that begins the story. **Write** a
sentence that could be in the middle of the story.
Write a sentence that could end the story.

Jack has a ball. **Possible answers:**

_____

4. Jack gives the ball to Mike._____

_____

5. They play a game._____

Home Activity This page helps your child identify the beginning, middle, and end of a story. Work through
the items with your child. Then ask your child to tell you different things he or she did today in the order that
they happened.

Name_____

Pick a word from the box to finish each sentence.
Write it on the line.

give   great   many   people

1. Max and Ann are kind **people** .

2. They **give** books to kids.

3. Ann is **great** at helping with pets.

4. Max likes to **give** food from his garden.

5. Max and Ann have **many** friends.

 Home Activity This page helps your child learn to read and write the words *give, great, many,* and *people.* Work through the items with your child. Help your child think of ways he or she can help around the house or in the neighborhood.

© Pearson Education A

Name_____

Finish each sentence.
Write the words on the lines.

<u>Possible answers:</u>

1. I can share <u>my truck</u> .

2. I can give <u>my mom a card</u> .

Write a sentence telling what you can share with a friend. **Write** your sentence on the line.

_____

3. <u>I can share my ball with Ted.</u>

_____

_____

Write a sentence telling how you can help at home. **Write** your sentence on the line.

_____

4. <u>I can give my dog a bath.</u>

_____

_____

© Pearson Education A

School + Home

Home Activity This page helps your child finish sentences and learn to write sentences. Help your child write the sentences. Then together, talk about other ways he or she can share with a friend or neighbor.

Name_____

Circle the word for each picture.

tall tall**er** tall**est**

1.

(faster) fastest

2.

(hotter) hot

3.

(bigger) biggest

4.

thicker (thickest)

5.

(sadder) saddest

6.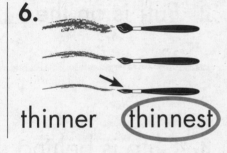

thinner (thinnest)

Write er or est to finish the word in each sentence.

Rose Lucy

7. Lucy has long ___**er**___ hair.

8. The little dog has the long ___**est**___ tail.

© Pearson Education A

School + Home **Home Activity** This page practices words ending with -er and -est that compare things. Work through the items with your child. Then look through magazines or catalogs together. Have your child compare people or objects using words with the -er or -est ending.

Name_____

Pick a word from the box to finish each sentence.
Write it on the line.

| bridge | budge | hedge | fudge | ledge |

1. Max is under the ___**bridge**___ .

2. Puff is on the ___**ledge**___ .

3. Chip is behind the ___**hedge**___ .

4. Our friends just won't ___**budge**___ .

5. Let's give them some ___**fudge**___ !

Home Activity This page practices words that end with *dge* that have the sound heard in *badge*. Work through the items with your child. Then have your child write the *dge* words from this page on a piece of paper. Work together to think of other words to add to the list.

© Pearson Education A

Name_____

Read each story. **Look** at the pictures.
Write 1, 2, 3 to show the right order.

Brent had a bike.
Brent rode too fast.
Brent hit a bump and fell.
Dad helped him to get up.

1. **2**  2. **3** 3. **1**

Min planted seeds.
She put them in the sun.
She gave them water.
The plants got bigger and bigger.

4. **3**   5. **1**   6. **2**

 School + Home **Home Activity** This page helps your child learn about the order in which events happen in a story. Work through the items with your child. Have your child tell you what he or she does to get ready for school in the morning. Ask what is done first, second, and third.

Practice Book Unit 5   **Comprehension** Sequence **125**

Name_____

Pick a word from the box to finish each sentence.
Write it on the line.

> away find long took

1. Ana __**took**__ her dog Tag to the park.

2. Tag ran __**away**__ when he saw a cat.

3. Ana looked for Tag for a __**long**__ time.

4. Ana had a great plan to __**find**__ Tag!

5. She called for Tag like a cat.

It didn't take __**long**__ for Tag to come running!

Home Activity This page helps your child learn to read and write the words *away*, *find*, *long*, and *took*. Work through the items with your child. Have your child think of words that rhyme with *find*, *long*, and *took*. Write the words and read them together.

© Pearson Education A

Name_____

Think of a problem you had.
How did you solve the problem?
Write the steps in the chart.

Problem

[ ]

Steps I Took

1. [ ]

↓

2. [ ]

↓

3. [ ]

↓

4. [ ]

Answers will vary but should include a problem and the steps that were taken to solve it. Steps should be in logical order.

Home Activity This page helps your child learn to write sentences that tell what happened in order. Help your child write the sentences. Cut apart the boxes with the sentences. Then mix up the sentences and have your child put them in the correct order.

© Pearson Education A

Name_____

Say the word for each picture.
Circle the word.

tr**ai**n    h**ay**

1.
(paint) park

2.
smell (snail)

3.
paid (play)

4.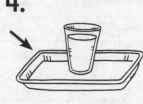
trip (tray)

5.
(rain) rake

6.
sad (sail)

7.
(pay) pail

8.
(nail) name

Circle the two words in each sentence that have the same **long a** sound as .

9. Buck likes to (wait) for the (mail).

10. He (stays) by the box all (day).

School + Home

Home Activity This page practices words with the long *a* sound spelled *ay* and *ai* heard in *stay* and *brain*. Work through the items with your child. Then have your child use the words from this page in a silly rhyme.

Name_____

Say the word for each picture.
Circle the word.

m<u>ea</u>t

1.	2.	3.	4.

(beans) bell	sell (seal)	jelly (jeans)	(steam) sick

5.	6.	7.	8.

tale (team)	(meal) miss	(peach) pat	class (clean)

Find the word that has the same **long e** sound as .
Mark the ⬭ to show your answer.

9. 🔘 beak   10. ⬭ tell
    ⬭ back   ⬭ trap
    ⬭ best   🔘 teach

 Home Activity This page practices words with the long e sound spelled *ea* heard in *dream*. Work through the items with your child. Then have your child use each word in a sentence.

Practice Book Unit 5   **Phonics** Long e: *ea* **129**

Name_____

Look at the pictures.
Write 1, 2, 3 to put the sentences in order.

1. Kate put ice cream in the glass. __1__

2. Kate ate her treat. __3__

3. She added some nuts. __2__

4. Then Ed trained Sam to beg. __2__

5. Ed trained his dog Sam to sit. __1__

6. Ed gave Sam treats after his tricks. __3__

 Home Activity This page helps your child put events in order to form a story. Work through the items with your child. Ask your child to draw a series of pictures showing three events in the order in which they happened.

Name_____

Pick a word to finish each sentence.
Write it on the line.

| don't   most   won't   write |

_____

1. When it is cold, __most__ kids stay inside.

_____

2. We __don't__ know what to do.

_____

3. We can __write__ a story.

4. We can bake a cake.

_____

We __won't__ make a mess!

_____

5. We can play __most__ games.

We can play hide and seek!

Home Activity This page helps your child learn to read and write the words *don't, most, won't,* and *write.* Work through the items with your child. Talk with your child about all the things he or she can do in the house on a rainy or snowy day.

© Pearson Education A

Name_____

Finish each sentence. **Write** the words on the lines.

1. What can I do?

Possible answers:

I can write a <u>poem for my teacher</u> .

2. What can I do?

I can make a <u>meal for my family</u> .

3. What can I do? I can find a <u>toy for my cat</u> .

4. What can I do for my friends?

<u>I can help my friends with homework.</u>

5. What can I do for my family?

<u>I can help my family with chores.</u>

© Pearson Education A

School + Home **Home Activity** This page helps your child learn to write sentences. Work with your child to write each sentence. Then together think of new ways your family can help each other. Try to think of one idea for each day of the week.

Name_____

Add **'s** or **'** to the end of each word.

cat**s'** dish  Kim**'s** cat

1. Chad __**'s**__ pet

2. girls __**'**__ kites

3. man __**'s**__ hat

4. dogs __**'**__ ball

5. jars __**'**__ lids

6. Brit __**'s**__ dress

Pick a word from the box to match each picture.
Write it on the line.

baby's   birds'

7. __birds'__ nests

8. __baby's__ blocks

 School + Home **Home Activity** This page practices words that show ownership. Work through the items with your child. Then walk around the house with your child, pointing out objects owned by one or more family members. Ask your child to use a word to tell you who owns each object, such as *Jen's lamp* or *the boys' bedroom*.

Name_____

Say the word for each picture. Circle the word.
Write it on the line.

m**ow**   s**oa**p

1.		bone	
		(bow)	**bow**
		be	

2.		(coat)	
		cot	**coat**
		code	

3.		bat	
		back	
		(boat)	**boat**

4.		(snow)	
		sap	
		stop	**snow**

5.		gap	
		got	
		(goat)	**goat**

Home Activity This page practices words with the long *o* sound spelled *oa* and *ow* heard in *toad* and *row*. Help your child write the long *o* words on this page on index cards. Ask him or her to sort the cards by their spellings.

Name_____

Look at both pictures. **Write** sentences to tell how the pictures are the same and different.

Ray

Jay

Same

Possible answers:_____

1. Ray and Jay are cats.

2. Ray and Jay are on rugs.

3. Ray and Jay are awake.

Different

1. Jay is standing and Ray is lying down.

2. Ray is white and Jay is black.

3. Ray has a hat, but Jay does not have a hat.

Home Activity This page helps your child write about how two things are the same and different. Work through the items with your child. Then ask your child to point out all the ways the two of you are the same and different.

Name_____

Read the sentence. **Unscramble** the letters. **Use** the words in the box. **Write** the word on the line.

| over | push | should | would |

1. I **ouwld** like some help.

   would

2. Put the word *dog* **vroe** that line.

   over

3. Now **shpu** "enter."

   push

4. You **holsud** look in this too.

   should

© Pearson Education A

Home Activity This page helps your child learn to read and write the words *over, push, should,* and *would.* Work through the items with your child. Then have your child use each word in a sentence.

Name_____

Look at the chart. Write words on the lines.
Keep your list.

Possible answers:

When I Need to Find an Answer

Where I Can Look	Who I Can Ask	What I Can Do
1. computer	4. teacher	7. try an experiment
2. book	5. parent	8. draw a picture
3. magazine	6. doctor	9. get help from a friend

Home Activity This page helps your child write a list of ways he or she can find answers to questions. Help your child fill in the chart. Then have your child tell you one question for which he or she wants an answer. Use the list to help your child find the answer.

School + Home

© Pearson Education A

Name_____

Change y to i.
Add -es and -ed to each word.
Write the new words on the lines.

cr**ies**   cr**ied**

	Add -es	Add -ed
1. try	tries	tried
2. spy	spies	spied
3. dry	dries	dried
4. fry	fries	fried

Change y to i. Add -er and -est to each word.
Write the new words on the lines.

	Add -er	Add -est
5. funny	funnier	funniest
6. lucky	luckier	luckiest

Home Activity This page practices adding endings to words in which the spelling changes from *y* to *i*. Work through the items with your child. Have your child add *-ed* to the words *hurry* and *study* and then use the new words in sentences.

© Pearson Education A

Name_____

Say the word for each picture. **Pick** letters from the box to finish each word. **Write** the letters on the lines.

stream

| scr | shr | spl | str | thr |

1. _____ **thr** ee

2. _____ **spl** ash

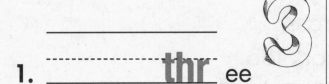
3. _____ **str** ing

4. _____ **scr** een

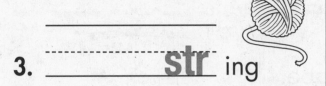
5. _____ **scr** ub

6. _____ **thr** one

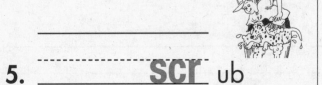
7. _____ **str** eet

8. _____ **shr** imp

9. _____ **thr** ow

10. _____ **str** ipe

School + Home

Home Activity This page practices words that begin with three-letter blends. Work through the items with your child. Then have your child name each picture and use each word in a sentence.

© Pearson Education A

Name _____

Read each story. **Find** the sentence that tells what the story is about. **Circle** that sentence. **Write** a title that tells what the story is about.

1. (Danny likes the park.)
   He likes to ride his bike there.
   He likes to play on the grass.
   He can fly a kite at the park too.

   Possible answer:
2. __Fun at the Park__

3. Fran got a big sheet.
   She got some yarn and tape.
   She got some pens.
   (Fran made a funny mask.)

   Possible answer:
4. __Fran's Mask__

5. (Sho cannot go to school.)
   (Sho is sick today.)
   He will stay in bed.
   Sho will get lots of rest.

   Possible answer:
6. __Sick at Home__

© Pearson Education A

School + Home **Home Activity** This page helps your child identify the main idea of a story. Work through the items with your child. Then have your child use his or her own words to tell you what each story is about.

Name_____

Pick a word from the box to finish each sentence.
Write it on the line.

| behind   love   pull   soon |

1. Min and Carl **love** to make things.

2. Min made a box to **pull** her bunny.

3. Carl made a box to **pull** his dog.

4. Min and Carl put the boxes **behind** them.

5. They **soon** go for a walk.

Home Activity This page helps your child learn to read and write the words *behind, love, pull,* and *soon.*
Have your child make up a sentence using each of the words.

© Pearson Education A

Name_____

Think of something that can make life easier. **Draw** a picture of it in the box. **Write** about it on the lines.

1.

> Picture should show an invention.

2. What will you call it?

_____

Answer should give a name
for the invention.

3. What can it do?

_____

Answer should tell what the invention can do.

4. Who will it help?

_____

Answer should tell who will be helped by the invention.

5. How will it make life easier?

_____

Answer should tell how the invention will make life easier.

© Pearson Education A

Home Activity This page practices writing sentences about an invention. Help your child write the sentences and read them. Then have your child look around your home for three inventions that make life easier.

Name_____

Circle a word to finish each sentence.
Write it on the line.

t**ie**

l**igh**t

---

nine (night)

_____

1. It gets dark at ___**night**___ .

(lie)   like

_____

2. We ___**lie**___ in our tent.

pay   (pie)

_____

3. We eat some ___**pie**___ .

his   (high)

_____

4. We look up ___**high**___ .

(bright)   bring

_____

5. The stars are ___**bright**___ .

Home Activity This page practices words with the long *i* sound spelled *ie* and *igh* heard in *die* and *sight*. Work through the items with your child. Have your child look at the page and find long *i* words that rhyme. (*light/night/bright* and *tie/lie/pie/high*)

© Pearson Education A

Name_____

Say the word for each picture.
Circle the word.

cand**le**

1.  (**bottle**)
   bone

2.  turned
   (**turtle**)

3.  (**needle**)
   needing

4.  (**table**)
   tab

5.  adding
   (**apple**)

6.  (**pickle**)
   picked

7.  pump
   (**puddle**)

8. 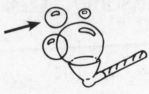 buddy
   (**bubble**)

Find the word that has the same ending sound as .
Mark the ⬭ to show your answer.

9. ⬭ ride
   ⬛ riddle
   ⬭ ring

10. ⬭ hang
    ⬭ handy
    ⬛ handle

© Pearson Education A

 School + Home **Home Activity** This page practices reading two-syllable words that end with *le*. Name each picture and work through the items with your child. Then write *little, middle, rattle,* and *tattle* and help your child read the words.

Name _____

Read the story.

Do you need to go on a trip? You can go in many ways. You can go by car. You can go on a ship. You can go on a train or plane.

---

1. **Circle** the big idea of the story.

   It is fun to go on a trip.

   (You can go places in many ways.)

2. **Circle** the best title for the story.

   (Many Ways to Go)

   A Long Trip

---

3. **Draw** a picture in the box to show the big idea.

   Pictures will vary.

4. **Write** a sentence that tells about your picture.

   Sentence should tell about the picture.
   _____
   _____
   _____
   _____
   _____

© Pearson Education A

School + Home **Home Activity** This page helps your child identify the main idea of a story. Work through the items with your child. Then ask your child to tell you how he or she would like to travel and why.

Pick a word from the box to finish each sentence.
Write it on the line.

| before   kind   none   sure |

_____
1. What __kind__ of car is that?

_____
2. We have not seen it __before__ .

_____
3. There are __none__ like that on our street.

_____
4. Here is the same __kind__ of car.

_____
5. It __sure__ looks fun to ride in!

© Pearson Education A

Name_____

Think about the way people did chores long ago.
Think about the way people do chores now.
Write your ideas on the lines.

Clean dirty socks and shirts
          Possible answers: _____

1. Then: <u>People cleaned at a stream.</u> _____

   _____

2. Now: <u>People use a washing machine.</u> _____

Make meals

3. Then: <u>People used fire.</u> _____

   _____

4. Now: <u>People use a stove.</u> _____

Go to the store

5. Then: <u>People had to walk.</u> _____

   _____

6. Now: <u>People can drive a car.</u> _____

 Home Activity This page practices writing sentences. Help your child write the sentences and then read them together. Ask your child to tell whether it is harder or easier to do chores now. Have your child explain his or her answer.

© Pearson Education A

Name_____

Drop the final **e.**
Add **-ed** or **-ing** to the word in ( ).
Write the new word on the line.

(make + ing)
_____

1. Becky is ___**making**___ a gift.

(wipe + ed)
_____

2. She ___**wiped**___ the can with a rag.

(glue + ed)
_____

3. She ___**glued**___ stars on the can.

(hope + ing)
_____

4. Becky is ___**hoping**___ that Dad will come soon.

(smile + ed)
_____

5. Dad took the gift and ___**smiled**___ .

Home Activity This page practices adding *-ed* and *-ing* to words that end in *e*. Work through the items with your child. Then write *bake* and *hike* on a sheet of paper. Have your child add *-ed* and *-ing* to each one and write the new words.

© Pearson Education A

Name_____

Say the word for each picture. Circle the word.

p**ony**

---

1.  wags (wagon)

2. (tiger) tile

3. some (sofa)

4. ripped (river)

---

5. (cabin) camp

6. (spider) spill

7. (robot) robe

8. came (camel)

Pick a word from the box to match each picture. Write it on the line.

⌈ **lemon   baby** ⌋

9.

_____ **baby** _____

10.

_____ **lemon** _____

© Pearson Education A

 School + Home   Home Activity This page practices two-syllable words that have one consonant in the middle. Name each picture. Work through the items with your child. Then have your child choose three words and use each one in a sentence.

Name_____

Read the story.

Tony looks in the mailbox. He sees a box. The box has his name on it! Tony opens the box. A car is inside. It is a gift from his uncle.

1. **Circle** the big idea of the story.

    (Tony gets a gift.)
    Tony sees a box.

2. **Circle** the best title for the story.

    A Funny Box
    (Tony's Gift)

Read the story.

Tony makes a ramp. He puts his car on top. Then he lets go. The car runs down the ramp. It is very fast! Tony plays again and again. His new car is a lot of fun!

3. **Circle** the big idea of the story.

    Tony likes to make ramps.
    (Tony has fun with his car.)

4. **Circle** the best title for the story.

    (A Fun Car)
    Time to Drive

5. **Write** a sentence telling what the two stories are about.

_____

Possible answer: Tony gets a new car and has fun with it.

_____

_____

© Pearson Education A

Home Activity This page helps your child identify the main idea of a story. Work through the items with your child. Then have your child imagine that the two stories come from one book. Ask your child to make up a title for the book.

Name_____

Pick a word from the box to finish each sentence.
Write it on the line.

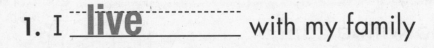

because   goes   live   school

1. I ____live____ with my family

2. Dad takes me to ____school____ each day.

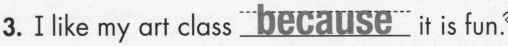

3. I like my art class ____because____ it is fun.

4. I made a plane at ____school____ .

5. My plane ____goes____ up high!

© Pearson Education A

School + Home

Home Activity This page helps your child learn to read and write the words *because, goes, live,* and *school.* Write each word on an index card and place the cards facedown. Have your child pick up one card at a time and read each word.

Name_____

Think of new ways you can use things.
Write your ideas on the lines.

1. What can you do with a box?

_____

Answer should tell how a box might be used.

2. What can you do with a can?

_____

Answer should tell how a can might be used.

3. What can you do with a sock?

_____

Answer should tell how a sock might be used.

4. Draw one of your ideas in the box.

Drawing should show one of the child's ideas.

5. Write a sentence about your picture.

_____

Sentence should describe the picture.

_____

© Pearson Education A

Home Activity This page practices writing sentences. Help your child write the sentences and read them together. Have your child choose one of the ideas on the page. Then have him or her tell you how to make the item.

Name_____

Words I Can Now Read and Write

_____   _____
------------------------   ------------------------
_____   _____
------------------------   ------------------------
_____   _____
------------------------   ------------------------
_____   _____
------------------------   ------------------------
_____   _____
------------------------   ------------------------
_____   _____
------------------------   ------------------------
_____   _____
------------------------   ------------------------
_____   _____
------------------------   ------------------------
_____   _____
------------------------   ------------------------
_____

_____

Name_____

Words I Can Now Read and Write

_____   _____

_____   _____

_____   _____

_____   _____

_____   _____

_____   _____

_____   _____

Name_____

I read _____

_____

It was about

Words I Can Now Read and Write

Name

I read

It was about

Words I Can Now Read and Write